Dayenu!

A Passover Haggadah
For Families and Children

By Carol Boyd Leon

Illustrated by Gwen Connelly

KTAV Publishing House, Inc.

Dedicated to my children – Sarah, Jacob and Jamie – for always having dreamed up the most innovative of hiding places for the afikomen! – *CBL*

Song lyric credits:
Ready for Passover (p. 3-6) by Carol Boyd Leon; *Shehecheyanu* (p. 8) by Carol Boyd Leon; *Building Cities* (p. 14) by Shirley R. Cohen; *Little Baby Moses* (p.16) by Carol Boyd Leon; *The Burning Bush* (p. 17) by Carol Boyd Leon; *Stubborn Pharaoh* (p. 18) by Carol Boyd Leon; *Frogs!* (p. 19) by Carol Boyd Leon; *Listen King Pharaoh* (p. 21) by Shirley R. Cohen; *Across the Sea* (p. 23) by Carol Boyd Leon; *Answering the Questions* (p. 25) by Carol Boyd Leon; *Birkat Hamazon* (p. 29) by Carol Boyd Leon; *Thank You God* (p. 31) by José Bowen; *Dayenu* (p. 32) English lyrics by Carol Boyd Leon.

DAYENU! CD TRACK LIST (CD IS INCLUDED IN SOME EDITIONS OF THIS HAGGADAH)

1.	Ready for Passover	Carol Boyd Leon	14.	Kadima	Folk song
2.	Candle Blessing	Traditional chant	15.	Across the Sea	Carol Boyd Leon
3.	Shehecheyanu	Traditional chant	16.	Avadim Hayinu	Shlomo Postolsky
4.	Shehecheyanu	Carol Boyd Leon	17.	Answering the Questions	Abileah / Leon
5.	Kiddush	Traditional chant	18.	Motzi-Matzah	Traditional chant
6.	Karpas	Traditional chant	19.	Bitter Herbs	Traditional chant
7.	Mah Nishtanah	Ephraim Abileah	20.	Birkat Hamazon	Carol Boyd Leon
8.	Building Cities	Shirley R. Cohen	21.	Eliyahu Hanavi	Traditional
9.	Little Baby Moses	Carol Boyd Leon	22.	Thank You, God	José Bowen
10.	The Burning Bush	Carol Boyd Leon	23.	Dayenu	Traditional
11.	Stubborn Pharaoh	Folk song / Leon	24.	1st Question Learning Track	– for Young Children
12.	Frogs!	Carol Boyd Leon	25.	4 Questions Learning Track	– for Older Children
13.	Listen King Pharaoh	Shirley R. Cohen	26.	4 Questions (instrumental)	

All songs © by the composers; blessings sung with Passover nusach. CD produced and narrated by Carol Boyd Leon; vocals by Carol Boyd Leon, Jamie Pierce Boyd, Jessica Campbell and the Dayenu Children's Choir; Adrian A. Durlester, accompanist.

Text copyright © 2008 by Carol Boyd Leon (ASCAP)

www.carolboydleon.com

KTAV PUBLISHING HOUSE, INC.
930 Newark Ave
Jersey City, NJ 07306 U.S.A.
201-963-9524
www.ktav.com

Printed in China

Library of Congress Cataloging-in-Publication Data

Leon, Carol Boyd.
Dayenu! : a Passover haggadah for families and children / by Carol Boyd Leon ; Illustrated by Gwen Connelly.
    p. cm.
  Text in English; portions of the Haggadah in Hebrew and romanized Hebrew with English translation.
  ISBN 978-1-60280-039-7 (32 page pbk.) — ISBN 978-1-60280-041-0 (64 page with sheet music added)
  1. Haggadah—Adaptations—Juvenile literature. 2. Seder—Juvenile literature. 3. Passover—Juvenile literature.
I. Connelly, Gwen. II. Haggadah. English & Hebrew. Selections. III. Title.
  BM674.76.L46 2008
  296.4'5371—dc22
                                 2008025641

LET'S GET READY FOR OUR SEDER

All text printed in blue can be sung.

We're glad that Spring has now arrived.
Nature seems to come alive.
The wind is blowing, the leaves are growing;
The grass will very soon need mowing!

Every Spring we can hardly wait
For Passover when we celebrate
By telling how it was that we,
The Jewish people, were set free.

Free to be like you and me;
Free like the fish swimming in the sea.
Free to be like you and me;
Free like the birds up in the tree.

We are getting ready to tell an important story about the Jewish people.

We set our table in a special way to help us tell the story.

Do we have everything we need?

For our seder, what do we need?

Haggadot for us to read,

Candles,

Kiddush cups,

A seder plate,

Three matzot —

Now let's celebrate!

Wait!

There's something else we need

To celebrate that we are free.

Can you guess what it might be?

Around the table...

...YOU AND ME!

We're all here, we're all here

To celebrate at this time of year.

We're all here, we're all here

To celebrate year after year!

WE are the ones who must tell the story.
WE are the ones who must listen,
learn and remember.

CANDLE LIGHTING

We begin our seder by lighting the holiday candles.

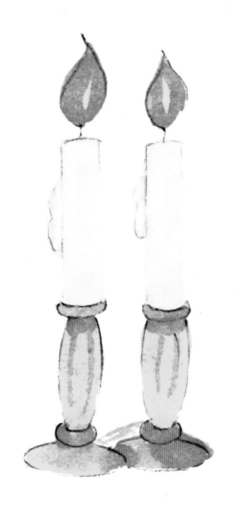

Light the candles.
On Shabbat, add the words in brackets.

בָּרוּךְ אַתָּה יְיָ
אֱלֹהֵינוּ מֶלֶךְ הָעוֹלָם
אֲשֶׁר קִדְּשָׁנוּ בְּמִצְוֹתָיו
וְצִוָּנוּ לְהַדְלִיק נֵר
שֶׁל [שַׁבָּת וְשֶׁל] יוֹם טוֹב:

Baruch atah Adonai
Eloheinu melech ha'olam
asher kid'shanu b'mitzvotav
v'tzivanu l'hadlik ner
shel [Shabbat v'shel] Yom Tov.

Blessed is Adonai our God, Ruler of the universe,
Who makes us holy with mitzvot and commands us
to kindle the [Sabbath and] holiday lights.

The holiday candles remind us that Passover
is a special time and a holy time.

We give our thanks to God for bringing us to this holiday.

בָּרוּךְ אַתָּה יְיָ אֱלֹהֵינוּ מֶלֶךְ הָעוֹלָם
שֶׁהֶחֱיָנוּ וְקִיְּמָנוּ וְהִגִּיעָנוּ לַזְּמַן הַזֶּה:

Baruch atah Adonai Eloheinu melech ha'olam
shehecheyanu v'kiy'manu v'higiyanu lazman hazeh.

Blessed is Adonai our God, Ruler of the universe,
for giving us life, for sustaining us, and for bringing us to this season.

Passover is a most special time of year.
We celebrate with family and friends so dear.
"Shehecheyanu" – that's what we say
For bringing us to this day!

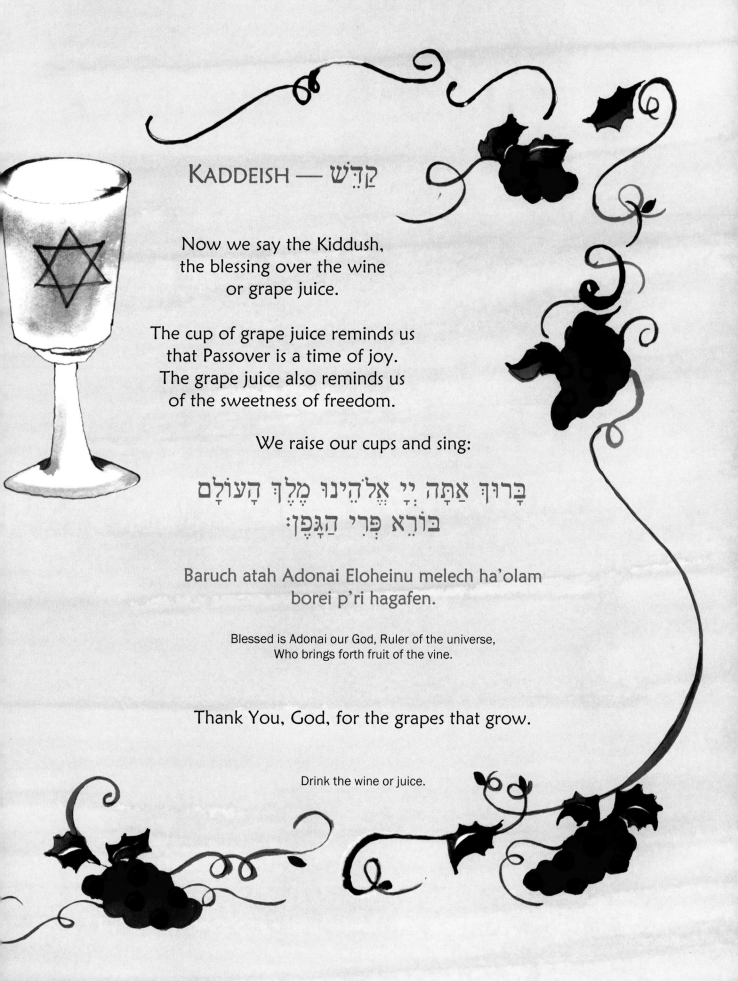

KADDEISH — קַדֵּשׁ

Now we say the Kiddush,
the blessing over the wine
or grape juice.

The cup of grape juice reminds us
that Passover is a time of joy.
The grape juice also reminds us
of the sweetness of freedom.

We raise our cups and sing:

בָּרוּךְ אַתָּה יְיָ אֱלֹהֵינוּ מֶלֶךְ הָעוֹלָם
בּוֹרֵא פְּרִי הַגָּפֶן:

Baruch atah Adonai Eloheinu melech ha'olam
borei p'ri hagafen.

Blessed is Adonai our God, Ruler of the universe,
Who brings forth fruit of the vine.

Thank You, God, for the grapes that grow.

Drink the wine or juice.

9

Our seder table has a seder plate with special food on it:

a bone called זְרוֹעַ (z'roa)

a roasted egg called בֵּיצָה (beitzah)

parsley or other greens called כַּרְפַּס (karpas)

chopped apples and nuts called חֲרֹסֶת (charoset)

and bitter herbs called מָרוֹר (maror)

PARSLEY — כַּרְפַּס (Karpas)

Give each person some parsley.

Spring is when new plants grow. It is a time of hope. Parsley reminds us that it was springtime when the Jewish people were freed from slavery. We dip the parsley that grew this spring into salt water. The salt water reminds us of the tears of the slaves and the tears of all people who are not free.

בָּרוּךְ אַתָּה יְיָ אֱלֹהֵינוּ מֶלֶךְ הָעוֹלָם
בּוֹרֵא פְּרִי הָאֲדָמָה:

Baruch Atah Adonai Eloheinu melech ha'olam
borei p'ri ha'adamah.

Thank You, God, for vegetables that grow in the ground.

Dip the parsley in salt water and then eat the parsley.

THE MIDDLE MATZAH — יַחַץ (Yachatz)

There are three matzot under the cover. We now uncover them, break the middle matzah in half and put one of the pieces — the larger one — away for dessert. The part that will be our dessert is called the *afikomen*.

We hide it in a safe place and find it after the meal.

Cover the remaining matzot.

THE FOUR QUESTIONS

Why is this night different from all other nights?

מַה נִּשְׁתַּנָּה הַלַּיְלָה הַזֶּה מִכָּל־הַלֵּילוֹת?

Mah nishtanah halailah hazeh mikol haleilot?

1

שֶׁבְּכָל־הַלֵּילוֹת אָנוּ
אוֹכְלִין חָמֵץ וּמַצָּה,
הַלַּיְלָה הַזֶּה כֻּלּוֹ מַצָּה:

Sheb'chol haleilot anu ochlin
chameitz u'matzah,
halailah hazeh kulo matzah.

On all other nights we eat all
kinds of bread and matzah.
On this night, why do we eat
only matzah?

2

שֶׁבְּכָל־הַלֵּילוֹת אָנוּ
אוֹכְלִין שְׁאָר יְרָקוֹת,
הַלַּיְלָה הַזֶּה מָרוֹר:

Sheb'chol haleilot anu ochlin
sh'ar y'rakot,
halailah hazeh maror.

On all other nights we eat all
kinds of vegetables and herbs.
On this night, why do we eat
bitter herbs — maror?

3

שֶׁבְּכָל־הַלֵּילוֹת אֵין אֶנוּ
מַטְבִּילִין אֲפִלוּ פַּעַם אֶחָת,
הַלַּיְלָה הַזֶּה שְׁתֵּי פְּעָמִים:

Sheb'chol haleilot ein anu matbilin
afilu pa'am echat,
halailah hazeh sh'tei f'amim.

On all other nights we don't usually
dip one food into another. Tonight
we dip parsley in salt water and bitter
herbs in charoset. On this night, why
do we dip twice?

4

שֶׁבְּכָל־הַלֵּילוֹת אָנוּ אוֹכְלִין
בֵּין יוֹשְׁבִין וּבֵין מְסֻבִּין,
הַלַּיְלָה הַזֶּה כֻּלָּנוּ מְסֻבִּין:

Sheb'chol haleilot anu ochlin
bein yoshvin u'vein m'subin,
halailah hazeh kulanu m'subin.

On all other nights, we eat sitting
up straight or reclining. On this
night, why do we recline?

We have asked four questions.
Where can we find the answers?
The Passover story can help us find them.

MAGGID — מַגִּיד
Telling the Story

Many, many years ago, the land of Egypt had a harsh ruler called Pharaoh. He forced the Jewish people who lived there to be his slaves. They had to work hard for Pharaoh making bricks and building cities. The lives of the Jewish people were very bitter.

Bang, bang, bang,
Hold your hammer low.
Bang, bang, bang,
Give a heavy blow.
For it's work, work, work
Every day and every night.
For it's work, work, work
When it's dark and when it's light.

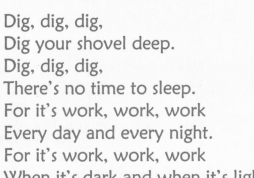

Dig, dig, dig,
Dig your shovel deep.
Dig, dig, dig,
There's no time to sleep.
For it's work, work, work
Every day and every night.
For it's work, work, work
When it's dark and when it's light.

Pharaoh was especially cruel to Jewish babies. To try to keep her baby safe, a Jewish mother placed her baby boy in a basket along the edge of the Nile River. The baby's sister, Miriam, watched to see what would happen.

Pharaoh's daughter, the princess, came to bathe in the river and found the basket with the baby inside. She called the baby "Moses" and decided to raise him like her own son. The Torah tells us that, in Egyptian, "Moses" means "brought out of the water."

Little baby Moses floating down the Nile,
Little baby Moses, will we see you smile?
Lying in a basket just like a little boat,
Lying in a basket which helps him stay afloat.

Baby Moses, baby Moses, baby Moses in the Nile.

The princess goes a-swimming in the river Nile.
The princess is the one who soon begins to smile.
The princess goes a-swimming and finds a baby boy.
What a happy princess, she now is filled with joy.

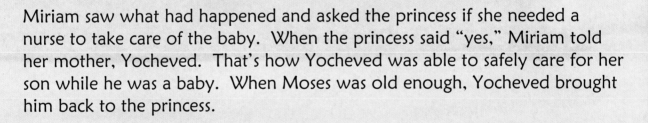

Baby Moses, baby Moses, baby Moses in the Nile.

She takes him from the water, then gives him a kiss.
She takes him from the water and kisses him like this.
She takes him from the water and kisses him once more.
She takes him from the water and brings him to the shore.

Baby Moses, baby Moses, Moses brought out of the Nile!

Miriam saw what had happened and asked the princess if she needed a
nurse to take care of the baby. When the princess said "yes," Miriam told
her mother, Yocheved. That's how Yocheved was able to safely care for her
son while he was a baby. When Moses was old enough, Yocheved brought
him back to the princess.

Although Moses grew up in the palace and was raised like a prince, he knew
that he was Jewish. One day, he saw Pharaoh's guard strike one of the
slaves. Moses struck back at the guard. Then Moses needed to leave Egypt
because he knew he would no longer be safe there.

Moses went to a faraway land and there he watched over sheep.

Moses was a shepherd when he saw a bush a-flame.
From that burning bush he heard God calling out his name.
"Moses, Moses, you must go to Pharaoh, don't you know?
You must tell the Pharaoh to let My people go!"

Let My people go! Let My people go!
You must tell the Pharaoh to let My people go!

If *you* heard a voice coming from
a burning bush, would you listen?

Moses returned to Egypt. He went to see Pharaoh as God had instructed. Moses said to Pharaoh, "Let my people go!" But Pharaoh would not agree.

Let's sing about what happened when Moses spoke to Pharaoh. Some of us can pretend to be Moses; others can pretend to be Pharaoh.

Sung to the melody of *I've Been Working On The Railroad:*

The Jews were building Pharaoh's cities
All the live-long day.
The Jews were working hard for Pharaoh
But they wanted to go and pray.
Moses went to meet with Pharaoh and said,
"Let my people go!"
Stubborn Pharaoh wouldn't listen;
To Moses, he said, "No!"

MOSES: Let my people go!   PHARAOH: No!

MOSES: Let my people go!   PHARAOH: No!

MOSES: God said to let
My people go, so
Let my people go!   PHARAOH: No!

MOSES: Let my people go!   PHARAOH: No!

MOSES: Let my people go!   PHARAOH: NO!!!

18

Moses told Pharaoh, "God said if you do not free the Jewish people, you will be punished." Pharaoh did not believe Moses even though Moses spoke the truth.

God became angry with Pharaoh and sent ten plagues to punish him.

First, the water turned to blood.

Next, there were frogs jumping everywhere!

Youngsters may want to get up from their seats and pretend to be those frogs.

Clap, clap, ribbit, jump!
Clap, clap, ribbit, jump!
Clap, clap, ribbit, jump!
Ribbit, jump, jump!

Frogs were in the palace.
Frogs were in the town.
Frogs were everywhere
A-jumping up and down.

Why so many frogs
Jumping everywhere?
God sent all those frogs
To get in Pharaoh's hair!

There were other plagues, too. For instance:

Cows got sick.
Fiery hail poured down.
Insects covered the land.
The sun did not shine for many days.

For older children:

We are sad that the Egyptians suffered from each plague and so
we take a drop of grape juice out of our cup as we name each one:

Blood	דָּם	*Dam*
Frogs	צְפַרְדֵּעַ	*Tz'fardeiah*
Lice	כִּנִּים	*Kinim*
Beasts	עָרוֹב	*Arov*
Cattle disease	דֶּבֶר	*Dever*
Boils	שְׁחִין	*Sh'chin*
Hail	בָּרָד	*Barad*
Locusts	אַרְבֶּה	*Ar'beh*
Darkness	חֹשֶׁךְ	*Choshech*
Slaying of the first born	מַכַּת בְּכוֹרוֹת	*Makat b'chorot*

Despite the plagues, Pharaoh remained stubborn and would not let the Jewish people go free.

MOSES: Oh listen, oh listen, oh listen King Pharaoh.
                  Oh listen, oh listen, please let my people go.
                  They want to go away. They work too hard all day.
                  King Pharaoh, King Pharaoh, what do you say?

PHARAOH: No! No! No! I will not let them go!
                  No! No! No! I will not let them go!

But after ten terrible plagues, Pharaoh was frightened and finally told Moses, "Take your people and quickly leave my land."

The Jewish people left Egypt in a hurry. They did not have time to bake bread for the long journey. Instead, they put bowls of raw dough on their shoulders and the sun baked it into matzah during their march forward – *kadima* – toward freedom.

Kadima, boom, boom, boom.
Kadima, boom, boom, boom.
Marching, marching out of Egypt, kadima.

Kadima, boom, boom, boom.
Kadima, boom, boom, boom.
Marching, marching to our freedom, kadima.

When they reached the sea, God told Moses
to hold up his walking stick. Nachshon was
the first to step into the sea.

Then a miracle happened! The water parted and the Jewish
people safely walked across on dry land to the other side.

But Pharaoh changed his mind and sent his soldiers to bring
the Jewish people back. When Pharaoh's soldiers tried to
cross the water, the sea closed upon them.

The Jewish people had a celebration because they were so happy to be free. Miriam played her tambourine and the people danced and sang songs of thanks to God for the miracle of their freedom.

One of the songs they sang was "Mi Chamocha" — Who is like You, God? There is none like you!

Come with me into the water.
Come with me across the sea.
Israel's sons and Israel's daughters,
Come with me; we're going to be free.

Forward, forward to our freedom,
Forward, forward through the sea.
Watch the water open for us.
God's own hand will set us free.

Mi chamocha ba'eilim Adonai?
Who is like You, Adonai?
There is none like You, our God,
Who opened up the sea
And helped us to be free.

God told the Jewish people to celebrate Passover every year
to remember that once we were slaves in Egypt, but now we are free!

עֲבָדִים הָיִינוּ, עַתָּה בְּנֵי חוֹרִין:

Avadim hayinu, hayinu
Ata b'nei chorin, b'nei chorin.
Avadim hayinu,
Ata, ata b'nei chorin.
Avadim hayinu
Ata, ata b'nei chorin, b'nei chorin.

We were slaves in Egypt, but now we're free.
We were slaves in Egypt, but now we're free.
We were slaves, we were slaves,
But now, but now, but now we're free.
We were slaves, we were slaves.
We were slaves in Egypt, but now we're free!

ANSWERING THE FOUR QUESTIONS

Can be sung to the *Mah Nishtanah* melody:
Here are the answers to our questions
1, 2, 3 and 4 (yes, 1, 2, 3 and 4).

1 We were rushing towards our freedom
So we could not wait for the bread to rise.
At Passover time, halailah hazeh
No bread for me, no bread for you,
Halailah hazeh, halailah hazeh
And also all week through.

2 Maror helps us remember that
The life of a slave is hard
And bitter as a bitter herb.
Halailah hazeh, halailah hazeh
We remember slavery,
Halailah hazeh, halailah hazeh
With maror for you and me.

3 Salt water is like the tears of slaves
And charoset is like the clay
We used to make the bricks.
Halailah hazeh, halailah hazeh
The parsley is dipped in salty water
Halailah hazeh, halailah hazeh
By every son and daughter.

4 We relax upon our chairs
As we recall the days
When we lived as slaves.
Halailah hazeh, halailah hazeh
We can lean back comfortably,
Halailah hazeh, halailah hazeh
Because we now are free.

"Halailah hazeh" means "on this night."

Sharing the Passover Food

Matzah — מַצָּה

We eat matzah to remember how the Jewish people left Egypt in a hurry and didn't have time to bake bread.

Give each person some matzah.

Together we say two blessings before eating the matzah:

בָּרוּךְ אַתָּה יְיָ אֱלֹהֵינוּ מֶלֶךְ הָעוֹלָם
הַמּוֹצִיא לֶחֶם מִן הָאָרֶץ:

Baruch Atah Adonai Eloheinu melech ha'olam
hamotzi lechem min ha'aretz.

בָּרוּךְ אַתָּה יְיָ אֱלֹהֵינוּ מֶלֶךְ הָעוֹלָם
אֲשֶׁר קִדְּשָׁנוּ בְּמִצְוֹתָיו וְצִוָּנוּ עַל אֲכִלַת מַצָּה:

Baruch Atah Adonai Eloheinu melech ha'olam
asher kid'shanu b'mitzvotav v'tzivanu al achilat matzah.

Thank You, God, for giving us bread
and for instructing us to eat matzah.

Eat the matzah.

26

BITTER HERBS — מָרוֹר (Maror)

Give each person some bitter herbs.

Bitter herbs, or maror, remind us of the bitterness of slavery.

בָּרוּךְ אַתָּה יְיָ אֱלֹהֵינוּ מֶלֶךְ הָעוֹלָם
אֲשֶׁר קִדְּשָׁנוּ בְּמִצְוֹתָיו וְצִוָּנוּ עַל אֲכִלַת מָרוֹר:

Baruch Atah Adonai Eloheinu melech ha'olam
asher kid'shanu b'mitzvotav v'tzivanu al achilat maror.

Thank You, God, for instructing us to eat bitter herbs.

Eat the maror dipped in charoset.

Some people make a "Hillel's sandwich" — maror and charoset between two pieces of Matzah...
although many children prefer a charoset-only sandwich.

THE EGG — בֵּיצָה (Beitzah) and
THE BONE — זְרוֹעַ (Z'roa)

Like the parsley, the egg on the seder plate reminds us that
spring is when the Jewish people were freed from slavery.
The bone reminds us that people roasted a lamb for the
first Passover celebration.

27

Now it's time for...

THE MEAL — שֻׁלְחָן עוֹרֵךְ (Shulchan Orech)

And then we search for

THE AFIKOMEN — צָפוּן (Tzafun)

Whoever finds the afikomen is rewarded.
The afikomen is then broken into pieces, distributed to all present and eaten.

Then Birkat Hamazon – the blessing after the meal (on next page) -- is sung.

BLESSING AFTER THE MEAL – בָּרֵךְ (Bareich)

To thank God for our food today,
This is the blessing that we say:

בָּרוּךְ אַתָּה יְיָ, הַזָּן אֶת־הַכֹּל:

Baruch atah Adonai hazan et hakol.

We give thanks for the food and land
Which we have with the help of God's hand.
Praised is God who gives life to us all.

Some seder tables have a
Miriam's Cup filled with water.

It is said that God gave Miriam a
miraculous well of water. The
well came with her through the
wilderness so the Jewish people
could have water during their
journey. Miriam's Cup helps us
remember Miriam and all that she
and other women have done to
keep the Jewish people alive.

ELIJAH'S CUP

Our seder table has an extra cup of wine. This cup is for Elijah,
a great Jewish teacher who lived many years ago.

People say Elijah visits every seder to wish everyone a year of peace.
Let's fill Elijah's cup and open the door to let Elijah in.

אֵלִיָּהוּ הַנָּבִיא, אֵלִיָּהוּ הַתִּשְׁבִּי
אֵלִיָּהוּ, אֵלִיָּהוּ, אֵלִיָּהוּ הַגִּלְעָדִי
בִּמְהֵרָה בְּיָמֵינוּ יָבֹא אֵלֵינוּ,
עִם מָשִׁיחַ בֶּן דָּוִד
עִם מָשִׁיחַ בֶּן דָּוִד:

Eliyahu hanavi, Eliyahu hatishbi,
Eliyahu, Eliyahu, Eliyahu hagiladi.
Bimhera b'yameinu yavo eileinu,
Im Mashiach ben David,
Im Mashiach ben David.

HALLEL — הַלֵּל

Now we sing and dance a song of praise
and thanks to God.

We'd like to thank God for the nose.
We'd like to thank God for the toes.
We'd like to thank You, God, for all our parts
And for all of the things we can do.

We can walk in a circle.
We can clap our hands.
We can jump up high.
We can roar!

We can stand up tall.
We can turn around.
We can wave our arms
And stamp the floor.

We'd like to thank God for the trees.
We'd like to thank God for the bees.
We'd like to thank You, God,
For the world You've made
And for letting us play in it, too.

Dayenu!

If God had taken us out of Egypt and done no more — DAYENU!
That would have been enough for us. But God did so much more.
God has given us so many gifts!

We conclude our seder by singing *Dayenu.*

אִלוּ הוֹצִיאָנוּ מִמִּצְרַיִם, דַּיֵּנוּ

Ilu hotzi, hotzi anu, hotzi anu mi-Mitz'rayim,
Hotzi anu mi-Mitz'rayim — dayenu!

Had God taken us from Egypt, only taken us from Egypt,
That would have been enough — it's dayenu!

אִלוּ נָתַן לָנוּ אֶת הַשַׁבָּת, דַּיֵּנוּ

Ilu natan, natan lanu, natan lanu et ha-Shabbat,
Natan lanu et ha-Shabbat — dayenu!

Had God given us Shabbat, only given us Shabbat,
That would have been enough — it's dayenu!

אִלוּ נָתַן לָנוּ אֶת הַתּוֹרָה, דַּיֵּנוּ

Ilu natan, natan lanu,
Natan lanu et ha-Torah,
Natan lanu et ha-Torah —
Dayenu!

Had God given us the Torah,
Only given us the Torah,
That would have been enough —
It's dayenu!

L'shanah haba'ah b'Yerushalayim!